THE
Silver Christmas Tree

A Holiday Adventure!

By ROBERT HONOR
Illustrations by Edel Ferri

The Silver Christmas Tree
Robert Honor

ISBN: 979-8-482535-00-4

Special thanks goes to Dorothy, Robin, Edel, and Robert

Publishing support and services provided by BirthaBookCoach.com
Contact info: Dorothy Holtermann, founder, dorothy@birthabookcoach.com

Cover design by Robin Locke Monda, robinlockemonda.com

Illustrations by Edel Ferri, Ferri Illustrations, el-fe.com

Page design by Robert Louis Henry

ROBERT HONOR is a graduate of Moravian College and New York University. He has taught screenwriting at The Tisch School of the Arts, authored the thriller, *Bogart's Hat*. Email: robert.honor@gmail.com

For Lorie, Jack, and Kav
and children of all ages

THE Silver Christmas Tree

A Holiday Adventure!

My little sister Lilly loves garlic as much as my friend Tommy Metz loves Oreos. I don't eat cookies at Tommy's house because Mrs. Metz offers us the ones she bakes. They taste like nothing, or sometimes when they taste like something, they taste like Reynold's Wrap. So, whenever I'm asked if I would like one I usually fib and politely say I don't like anything sweet. Mr. Metz once said my teeth would live beyond the grave. It sounds like a compliment, except when he says it he sounds like Count Dracula. And he says it every single time I say *no thank you* to a cookie.

Now, my mother, she can make anything out of anything. She's especially good at baking things. Mother cleans other people's houses when they tell her they have company coming over. She never works on Friday. On Friday afternoons, after the whistle blows at the school yard, Mother greets us and we all walk to the market together. Lilly is the slowest walker because she likes to count the cracks on the sidewalk. This time, on our way to the market, Lilly, paying too much attention to the pavement, walks straight into a telephone pole. She's more upset than hurt because she can't remember how many cracks she's counted. Mother takes off her gloves and rubs soft, warm hands over Lilly's face and makes her feel better. I know her hands are soft and warm because, once in a while, she holds my face in her hands. Whenever she does it, it looks to me like she's thinking about writing a poem. Mother whispers to Lilly that she's going to look like a unicorn princess. As Mother speaks to her, the bump on her forehead seems to grow bigger and bigger, like in the cartoons. Maybe I'm making that up.

At the market Mother scrambles the pennies and nickels in her purse with her finger and buys handfuls of garlic that the grocer, the man named Tom, who has a mustache that looks like a walrus's whiskers, explains "is on its way out."

He says the same thing every week, "It's on the way out, but if you want it I'll take something off the top." *Take something off the top*, when he says it he sounds like the barber, Mr. Browne, who has an *e* at the end of his name.

As usual, the garlic is brown and soft and a little gooey, and after he coughs and sneezes out all the stuff hiding in his mustache, Tom the grocers says to Mother, if she cooks spaghetti on Saturdays instead of every Friday, he would gladly give her garlic for free every Saturday morning. On Saturdays we usually have homemade butter cookies and jam sandwiches for a snack, and scrambled eggs made with whatever is leftover in the Frigidaire as our supper. The leftovers with eggs, my mother calls this giambote. Besides the garlic Mother buys a quart of milk with a smaller picture of the cow on it than the gallon of milk has, some walnuts, cinnamon and the white stuff, flour.

On our way home we pass the five and dime, where my steps are slow because I'm staring at the most amazing thing that I have ever seen: a silver Christmas tree. It's in the window and stands straighter than Robby the robot. It's taller than the Rifleman and it has a glow coming from it I have never seen before—not even treasure inside a pirate's chest can compare. Maybe I'm telling a little bit of a fib or exaggerating. Mr. Johnson, the owner of the store, makes eye contact with Mother. He's inside the store dusting his apron off with his big hands. His fingernails are black.

"Come Charlie, pay attention to where you're walking. Only one unicorn to a house," Mother says in an almost-serious voice.

"And only one princess," Lilly shrieks.

"Oh, okay Mother," I hear myself say in a small voice. "I wish we had a tree like this one." I see my mother's face change immediately; I wish I hadn't said anything at all.

"Me too," cries Lilly. "Beautiful creatures like a unicorn deserve to have a beautiful Christmas tree."

"Oh, is that so, Lilly?" my mother says, the happiness returns to her cheeks.

I think I see my mother laughing at Lilly, but she hides her amusement behind one of the gloves she forgot to put back on. She fixes Lilly's collar and makes sure my cap is on straight.

"Put your hands over your ears like muffs, Charlie, so they don't get cold," she says. She slips her hand into her glove and we all march for home. I can't stop thinking about mechanical men from Mars, pirates fighting over treasure and the silver Christmas tree.

The next morning Lilly and I wake up at the same time, excited. Not only is it Saturday—it's Christmas Eve! Our bedroom door opens. Mother is wearing the same dress she had on the day before, but somehow it looks brand new. She has a way of making everything look bright. I overheard one of the ladies on the avenue say she was a magician.

"Oh, somebody's been eating the leftover garlic again," Mother says waving a hand in front of her face.

"Don't look at me," I say sounding like one of the Bowery Boys.

Lilly's side of the room smells like gymnasium socks. I have garlic tears in my eyes, and it feels like I have garlic smoke up my nose. Mother sits on Lilly's bed and looks at her bump like the school nurse looks at the pimple that won't go away on the end of Tommy Metz's nose, except Mother doesn't make the sourpuss face. Mother was a nurse in the old country. She says she's going to be a nurse again someday, when she gets all of her ducks in a row.

Lilly's bump is nearly gone, now it's surrounded by the colors of the rainbow. The rainbow part are my mother's words. Lilly giggles.

Mother kisses Lilly on the head and says, "Now remember, next Friday those same cracks will still be there. You have to promise me that you'll walk with your head and eyes up." Lilly nods and smiles. I know she plans on doing exactly the same thing, hopefully without bumping into the telephone pole. Mother points to me and tells me to brush my teeth. To Lilly she says with a smile, "You have to brush yours twice."

Pop comes in and messes the hair on my head and he kisses the tiny bump on Lilly's head without really touching her with his lips. I suppose he doesn't want to hurt her. He says goodbye to us, squeezes Mother's hand, and then sighs. He doesn't say anything to her, but when he looks at her, his eyes twinkle. He turns and leaves for work wearing the white shirt with his name on it. It's a name I've never heard before or read anywhere, not in the movies or in the comic books. His name is Elio. Every night when Pop comes home from work he fills the kitchen sink with Javel, which is bleach and makes his white shirt swim around in it for a while.

Mother takes it out of the sink and puts it over the radiator to dry. She irons it in the morning and then he goes to work again. Sometimes he works two shifts.

Pop is a quiet man. He doesn't speak much. I heard Mr. Metz once say that my pop speaks pigeon English, and that doesn't sound like a compliment to me. Lilly and I and Mother have no trouble understanding him. After we wash up and brush our teeth we rush into the living room and stare at our Christmas tree. Lilly makes a face like she's having a sour ball.

"Oh, well," she says in neither a sad or a happy voice.

Our Christmas tree is about three-feet high and it's dug into a clay pot sitting on the side table. It looks droopy, as if Tom the grocer has been coughing and sneezing on it all day long. It has silver tinsel falling over it. The things that make it happier are the jams and cookies and bread that Mother makes so well, which surrounds it, in many small dishes.

Lilly and I spend most of the day climbing the smaller trees in the yard and kicking a ball around, praying for snow, and hoping for a glimpse of Santa. We both know that's a long shot. Mother comes outside several times to check on Lilly, and when it's time to return inside she tells us she has some warm Bosco waiting for us.

At bedtime I watch my mother run her hands through Lilly's hair until she falls asleep. When she sits on the edge of my bed I tell her, "Mother, every single boy and girl in my class says Santa Claus isn't real." She sighs like my pop when he had to leave her in the morning.

"*Is* Santa Claus a real person or someone in a storybook?" I ask. "I have a feeling I know what your answer is going to be."

"Well, there is a little Christmas in all of us," she says, trying not to frown.

"You mean…?"

"I mean to say, there is a little Santa Claus in all of us."

I moan, "Okay, oh boy, I had a feeling," I say to her. "I guess the same goes for the Tooth Fairy and the Easter Bunny then?"

"Don't let it spoil your dreams, Charlie." she says. "You're growing up and you'll soon learn that the best stories come from inside here," she says tapping on the place where her heart is, "and here," she points to my head where I suppose my brain is. "Now go to sleep. Your pop's already asleep. He's had a long day. And none of this Santa business with Lilly."

I wake up talking in my sleep, but I'm not sure what I'm saying. Our bedroom door is open. On very cold nights my parents leave the door open, so the heat can breathe throughout the whole house. The house is dark and so quiet I can hear the alarm clock ticking away in my parent's bedroom. Pop is snoring. I hear a click toward the front of the house. I jump out of bed right into my slippers. I sneak out of my room. I spy my mother wrapped in her winter coat and kerchief leaving the house. I can't make out the time on the clock above the kitchen sink, but the hands look to be in nowhere land, meaning it's especially late. I pull one of Pop's sweaters off the coat rack and put it on. It fits me like a king's long-flowing robe. I have to be careful not to trip over myself.

The sky is black, and the clouds looks heavy, like they're about to burst. I follow my mother outside. It looks like she's heading for the avenue. She's walking fast, and my toes are already cold inside my slippers. They aren't meant to see this kind of action, my toes or my slippers.

The streets are quieter than ever. Christmas lights in the store windows are inviting. Even the places that no kid likes to go to—the hardware store, the Yellow Cab office, the dentist—look cheerful. I think I hear a rumble in the sky. I look up and the only thing I notice: there's no Santa, no sled, and no reindeer bursting through the clouds.

There is one taxi cab parked by the curb outside the office. My mother passes the taxi and continues. As I pass, I see Mr. Rollo asleep inside his cab with a lit cigar in his mouth. I scoot by before the ash drops onto his tie.

I follow Mother to an alleyway behind the five and dime. A back door opens and light spills outside. After taking a good look at Mr. Johnson, my mother looks uncertain and suddenly cold. Mr. Johnson wobbles as he leans a tall cardboard box against the alley wall.

"Twelve dollars and thirty-seven cents. Fifty percent off. That was the agreement, Mr. Johnson. Thank you, sir." She speaks quickly. I understand why. Mr. Johnson looks like he's drunk.

"Well, that was the prior agreement Mrs. DelPriore, but I've had a change of heart."

"A change of…I don't understand. I have the money right here. I'll give you thirteen dollars. I think that's fair considering our earlier conversation."

"I don't know now. I could just as well hang onto it and make my money next Christmas. Full-price money, you know."

My mother removes folded dollars from her pocketbook and offers it to Mr. Johnson.

"You know, perhaps if you people—meaning your husband and yourself—perhaps if you worked harder, you could afford to pay the full price like everybody else."

Mother throws the money at Mr. Johnson. Her body becomes still as she stares at her hard-earned money on the ground. I know it's hard-earned money because she always tells me so.

"I'm going to take my money and leave now, Mr. Johnson."

"You may certainly leave Mrs. DelPriore but leave the money. Consider it the price of admission."

Mother marches out of the alley. I press my back against another doorway and hide as best I can. I watch as she runs by. I've never seen her run before. I've never seen her angry, not like this, and now I'm angry too.

I hear Mr. Johnson laughing. He sounds like a sloppy dog slurping water from a bowl. Picking the money off the ground, he nearly tips over. He stumbles back inside the five and dime. I hear the inside bolt being pulled. I'm smiling to myself because he's forgotten the cardboard box. I have a feeling I know what's inside. I wiggle my toes inside my slippers to make sure they're still alive. As I make my way toward the cardboard box, it begins to snow.

But now I have a big problem, I tell myself. How am I going to get home before Mother? I grab the box and drag it out of the alley, pulling it by the twine that's keeping it closed. I can see Mother up ahead. She passes Mr. Rollo's cab and makes a turn. I knock on Mr. Rollo's window. It takes a few seconds for him to wake up and gather himself. He looks at me like I'm a rabbit that just got pulled out of a magician's hat.

"Little Charlie, do you have a secret rendezvous with Sanny Claus? What are you doing out here at this hour?"

I don't have the heart to tell him the truth about Santa Claus, the Easter Bunny or the Tooth Fairy. I'm pretty sure he knows. Mr. Rollo keeps looking at his watch like it's a mistake and he continues talking while sweeping away the fallen ash on his skinny tie. I don't mean to be rude, but I'm running out of time and so I interrupt him, and I tell him the story of my mother, Mr. Johnson and a deal gone sour.

"Sounds just like Johnson. The ole bait and switch."

"Can you get me home fast, Mr. Rollo, before my mother?" I plead.

"You got the right man for the job kid. Get in."

"I don't have any money."

"Oh, what's dough? We're going on an adventure."

"Thank you, Mr. Rollo," and then I tell him which way my mother is going so he can take the back way.

"High Ho Silver kid and hang tight," he says winking at me. "We're in for a slippery ride. Will you look at this snow, Charlie? Isn't it wonderful?"

"Yes, Mr. Rollo, it is." I sneezed, and I sneezed again.

I hear voices and I feel Lilly jump onto my bed.

"Get up silly, it's Christmas! And it's snowing buckets."

My feet are cold under the covers and it's hard to open my eyes. Pop follows Lilly in and mushes the mattress with his hand. When I don't get up I hear him call my mother's name. I'm out of the bed by the time Mother enters the room. They're both looking at me like I'm from outer space.

Mother feels my head and says, "he's warm."

"I feel fine," I say. "Let's have Christmas. I heard a rumor that it snowed."

Before I'm allowed to join everyone in the living room, Mother gives me a dose of medicine from a tablespoon.

"Where are your slippers?"

"I don't know," I mumble to her. I put them behind the radiator to dry, but I can't tell her that. Mother leaves my room and returns with a pair of Pop's big wooly socks. She puts them over my cold feet.

We gather around the droopy Christmas tree, which looks happier than it did the day before. There are presents for Lilly and for me. An Annie Oakley vest and some coloring books for her; some marbles and a Lone Ranger's mask for me. I think about Mr. Rollo's *Hi Ho Silver* and smile. Mother brings out some warm Bosco and her famous cinnamon walnut bread. She and Pop take turns sipping black coffee and holding hands.

I decide it's time for me to present them with my surprise, but there's a heavy knock at the door. It's Mr. Metz in his policeman's uniform, looking bored and tired and Mr. Johnson looking just as dopey as he did the last time I saw him.

Mr. Johnson begins barking the second Mother opens the door.

"Where is it, Mrs. DelPriore?"

"Where is what, Mr. Johnson?" she says with some of the same anger I witnessed in her last night, in her voice now.

"Mrs. DelPriore, I'm sorry to bother you on Christmas morning, but Johnson says you took a Christmas tree from his store," says Mr. Metz, not looking at anyone.

"Took? Stole you mean, stole," Mr. Johnson says.

I see the muscles in Pop's forearms get crunchy and his eyes are not twinkling when he glares at Mr. Johnson. Mr. Johnson takes one step back.

"Wait a minute," I say in a big voice I don't recognize. "I'll be right back."

"Charlie?" I hear my mother say behind me. She doesn't sound like herself either.

I run into the cold room. It's the room to the one side of the kitchen, not much bigger than a closet. It has no radiators. Mother usually puts things in there in the winter, to keep, she says. Leftovers if we have any, or anything else that doesn't fit inside our small Frigidaire. I grab the cardboard box and drag it toward the front door. When I finally look up I see the odd expressions on everyone's faces with the exception of Lilly, who looks like she just found her lollipop.

"What's in the box?" asks Lilly sounding like a unicorn princess. "A train set?"

Before anyone else can say anything, I say to Mr. Metz in a commanding voice, "My mother bought it from Mr. Johnson fair and square."

"Charlie…?" my mother says looking confused; still not sounding like herself.

Mr. Metz asks Mr. Johnson, "Is it true Johnson, she bought it?"

"Well sort of, well no." Mr. Johnson was beginning to look like a cartoon locomotive about to run off the track.

"He wanted twelve dollars and thirty-seven cents," I say.

"And did you get it, Johnson?" asked Mr. Metz. "Did you get your money?"

"He took a full thirteen dollars," I say, taking a bite out of one of Mother's cookies. Mr. Metz looks oddly at me. He figures out what he probably knows inside, that his wife makes rotten cookies. Mr. Metz looks away from me and glares at Mr. Johnson. "You asked for twelve thirty-seven, but you took thirteen? And we're standing on these good people's doorstep letting the cold in on this Christmas morning accusing them of what?"

"You don't know the full story, Metz."

"I think I do, Johnson. You made a deal, had a few nips too many and then you got creative—or shall I say greedy. Wait for me in my car."

Mr. Johnson huffs and puffs, and bubbles some spittle onto his lower lip. He stomps away.

Mr. Metz removes his hat and says, "I am so very sorry, but I'll tell you what, I'm about to get a thirteen-dollar donation from Johnson there, and it will be returned to you for all the trouble he's caused.

"That's not necessary," Mother says. "We have our silver Christmas tree."

"Oh, indeed, it is necessary," Mr. Metz says.

"Would you like a cup of coffee?" Pop says to Mr. Metz very clearly. Mr. Metz looks surprised and maybe a little ashamed of himself. "I'll take a raincheck, sir. Thank you very much." He and Pop shake hands.

Mr. Metz asks Mother, "Mrs. DelPriore, do you think you can take a look at that thing on the end of Tommy's nose? The school nurse doesn't know what to make of it?"

"Certainly," Mother says. "I'm sure it's nothing to worry about."

Lilly waves goodbye to the police car and I watch Mother and Pop remove the silver Christmas tree from the box from my place under the warm blankets on the couch. Mother lectures me for following her out

into the cold; Pop pretends to be mad at me for rescuing the tree. As Lilly and Pop began to put the tree together Mother edges herself next to me on the couch.

"See, there is a little Santa in you, Charlie," she whispers, sounding very much like herself. "I was right."

"And a little Santa in Mr. Metz, too," I say.

"In Mr. Metz, too," she repeats.

"And Mr. Rollo. He was my sidekick, or maybe I was his sidekick."

"When you're feeling better you can take some cookies over to Mr. Rollo."

"I don't feel so disappointed knowing there's no real Santa Claus, now that I know how good other people can be."

"That's a grown-up thing to say," Mother says.

There is something else on my mind. "Is there supposed to be a little Tooth Fairy in me too?" I ask. "Because Lilly has a lot of baby teeth left and I don't have that kind of money."

I feel myself drifting asleep after all the excitement. When I wake up, Lilly is tapping on my bedroom window. She's in the backyard, looking funny because she's so bundled up and wobbly-looking. She can barely take small steps in her winter clothes without making herself giggle. Her cheeks are a strawberry red and she looks as happy as I have ever seen her.

"Look, look over here...." She points to the snow on the ground.

Without having to lift my head from the pillow I can see tiny footprints in the snow. Lots of them; so many that my imagination begins to race straight toward the North Pole. Behind the footprints there's an outline of a...sled?

"And Charlie, look up there! In the sky."

I stumble out of bed and press my nose against the cold window pane. Lilly is pointing into the sky. There's a jumble of clouds taking shape; they look like Santa Claus and his reindeer, streaking across the sky in slow-motion.

"Charlie?" I hear my mother call from the living room. She sounds very confused.

The front door bursts open and Lilly tumbles inside on her wet snow boots. Pop catches her and picks her up.

"Wow! Ooh! Look, Look Charlie!"

The silver Christmas tree is surrounded by dozens of magically wrapped presents. With ribbons and bows that sparkle. The tags say, Mother, Father, Charlie and Lilly. Lilly wiggles in Pop's arms. My mother puts her arm around me. She looks like she's glowing with happiness.

"Santa paid us a super special visit, Mother!" Lilly announces. "A very, very, special delivery."

I look up to my mother and say, "I do believe there's a little bit Santa in all of us. I think Santa believes it too. And we do have to have another talk about the Tooth Fairy. But not today."

END

ROBERT HONOR is a graduate of Moravian College and NYU. He taught screenwriting at The Tisch School of the Arts for fifteen years. Besides *The Silver Christmas Tree*, Robert is the author of the mystery/thriller, *Bogart's Hat*. His one-act plays have been performed in New York City; he's working on a *Bogart's Hat* sequel and a standalone thriller: *Brooklyn Bound*, set in 1955. He lives in the NYC area with his family, their Great Dane, Pinkie, and their kitty, Stinky.

Made in the USA
Middletown, DE
11 November 2021